Quotes Birthed Out of the Revelation of God's Glory

Enigmatic Proverbs

Rebecca L. King

Dedication

I would like to dedicate "Quotes Birthed Out Of The Revelation Of God's Glory" to the two greatest people that I know. Your expressions of love and patience towards me have proven to be some of the most influential ingredients in my life. Thank you both for exemplifying the eternal truths of God and allowing me to take the time necessary to find it on my own. The little things that you taught me have had a large impact on all of my newly discovered abilities. Thank you for encouraging and upholding me throughout my life, but especially in this last season while walking under the revelation and glory of God. May He bless you both with peace, joy and longevity. Not only are you the best friends that I have ever had, but you are also the best parents I have ever had! I love you both greatly.

Johnny and Marie King

Endorsement

As I read these quotes, I feel an awesome respect for the Author that took the time and effort to pen these life-giving words. Rebecca has lead us on an amazing journey into the depths of God's word over the last couple of years, and this book sums up everything we have learned. These are quotes that move you and help you understand all that you have learned in a simplistic but direct way.

It was only after experiencing the extraordinary encounter with God at the well that she became enlightened to the thoughts and desires of God that is upon all of our lives. The open revelation from Heaven that she operates in gives us new meanings of old sayings. Her words express the greatness of God but in a way that I can understand and appreciate the true intimacy, he desires with me. Quotes have long been the way to my heart and this book is full of insights, promises, and conditions that will bring you into the wholeness God desires for each one of his children.

This book is a treasure to behold and anyone who reads it will forever be changed if they apply these quotes in their day-to-day living. The concepts of the quotes answer the questions of life that can set your soul free and help you understand what the Glory of God represents in our everyday lives. I would recommend this book to all that are hungry to know the heartbeat of God, and desires their life to be in rhythm with his. Be encouraged as you read Quotes Birthed Out Of the Revelation of God's Glory as your daily inspiration and be blessed.

Marie King, *Mother of Rebecca King*

Forward

On March 19, 2010, I encountered an orchestrated introduction to Rebecca King, by the tender hand of our Heavenly Father. We met just thirty-four days after her experience at the well, where she discovered true intimacy with a Holy God and His glory. As I have watched Rebecca over the last three years, I have seen the intensity of the Glory of God birth forth revelation as she ministers under the cloud of His presence. She becomes engulfed in the flames of fire as His presence saturates and envelopes her, and fills the very room which changes the atmosphere with His greatness, splendor, magnificence, illumination, and divine presence.

To many she is Rebecca King, founder and C.E.O. of Harvest Time International Ministries. To others, she is recognized for establishing a children's home called The House of David. But to those close around her, she is Rebecca, His beloved, the one who carries His presence as she dwells under His wings. Revelation is unveiled from the Throne of Heaven as He whispers into her very being.

She is a great storyteller and teacher of parables, using boldness, straight-forwardness, and humor. Her listeners sit with great anticipation as she pours forth the revelation given straight from God. She walks with great authority while under the mantle of His glory.

It has been an honor to sit in her presence and see what God has done in one woman who gave her agenda over to her Father and said, "Not my will, but your will." It is a privilege to witness each morning, as she sits and waits in His presence, and to hear what her day utters for her assignment to be for the Kingdom of God on that day.

This book is a collection of quotes that were birthed under revelation, and they are His words to you: His beloved. I exhort you to take these quotes and make prayers out of them as a declaration over yourself. Allow them to come alive and do a new thing in your life! Let them enter into the deep crevices of your being, the very area you thought you had kept hidden, and let the life, illumination, and the God of Glory come in and set you free from yourself.

Quotes Birthed out of the Revelation of God's Glory will awake you to the answers that you have been searching for, but didn't think you could find. You will see yourself, along with the situations and circumstances of your life, in these pages and know you are not the only one who feels this way. But my friend, as you read each page, you will find the missing pieces, which are these enigmatic proverbs.

And now, dear reader, I declare blessings over those who read this book; that you would find peace, answers, intimacy, destiny, and a life full of adventures and His presence. May you become ignited with the fire and glory of a Holy God, and receive a life change into you and your very atmosphere! I pray that the God of our Lord Jesus Christ, the Father of glory, give unto you the spirit of wisdom and revelation in the knowledge of Him, and the eyes of your understanding be enlightened as you ponder these enigmatic proverbs. May you walk into your destiny, and come to know the true end and scope of life which is the King of Glory.

Gail Gaskins

Table of Contents

Revelation and Glory

- The glory of God is the convincing manifestation of God's presence.

- The glory is who He is. The revelation is what He says.

- Revelation is God's explanation.

- Revelation gives you an eternity of truth.

- Revelation reveals hidden mysteries.

- The revelation of God reveals the intentions of God.

- The glory is transferable.

- When you acknowledge the glory of God, even the patriarchs of old come to your attention.

- The glory of God makes you whole.

- When you are under His glory, you see things differently. You begin to see yourself as He sees you.

- The veil of ignorance has kept us from seeing and hearing God's glory.

- You will never be changed by the glory, unless you acknowledge God's glory.

- Under the glory, you are not as hard on yourself.

- Human comprehension cannot touch the glory.

- The glory introduces you to true intimacy.

- You have to have faith to receive revelation.

- When the glory comes down, it is heaven invading earth.

- The glory of God fills all emptiness.

- You have to make yourself available for the glory.

- The glory of God is for seekers and givers.

- The glory changes seasons in the natural and in the supernatural.

- Under the glory, evil schemes are exposed.

- The glory releases religion and demonstrates relationship.

- The glory introduces you to change and transformation.

- If you desire change in your life, you must make room for His glory.

- Moses saw the glory on the burning bush. You will always see the glory before it sets you free.

- Humility births revelation.

- Revelation reveals the truth.

- Revelation becomes truth when it is heard.

- The glory will validate all of your invalidations.

- The glory of God will unveil and expose you.

- Judgment will keep you from His glory.

- To carry the glory, you must carry the mantle of humility.

- What evil tries to conceal will be revealed in the glory.

- The cloud of confusion is the counterfeit to the glory cloud of God.

- The closer that you get to His throne, the more the enemy's voice sounds like His own.

- The glory crushes deception.

- Wisdom is God's thoughts.

- Wisdom brings automatic authority.
-
- Knowledge married to understanding brings forth wisdom.

- Knowledge is what we receive as we travel in truth.

- The glory will eradicate your fears.

- Revelation is like quick sand; if you get in it, you go deep quick.

- The glory of God will make you transparent. The evidence of your transparency depends upon the truth and power that resides within you.

- The supernatural needs to become natural to us, where we won't be shocked by signs, wonders and miracles.

- Revelation will revolutionize your life.

- Under the glory of God, you will be able to hear other people's thoughts.

- The glory is in the elements of God; Wind. Fire. Water. Earth.

- The glory brings both visitation and revelation.

- The glory illuminates truth and exposes darkness.

- The glory forces you to see yourself.

- The glory will take you out to bring you in.

- Creation is God's glory in action.

- Creative miracles are in the atmosphere of the glory.

- The glory makes you transparent from the enemy.

- You cannot have self-pity and the glory at the same time.

- The glory comes to take you into an intoxicating place of intimacy.

- When God sends forth His glory, it has to be received. If not received by man, then the elements swell to give Him the glory.

- The glory brings forth intimacy, not insecurities.

- Excellence will always ensure the glory of God.

- The glory will expose the schemes and plans of the enemy in your life.

- The glory will also expose the schemes of others in your life.

- When you are under the glory cloud of God, it has to be His way over yours.

- The glory is not a feeling, it's a healing.

- Revelation has no emotions, it is stable and fixed.

- Revelation reveals God's intentions.

- The glory of God draws curses out from where they have been stuck to manifest them; it's up to you to break them.

- The glory in you that acknowledges the glory of God produces illumination.

- Revelation is like a sharp knife that cuts.

- The revelation God gives for our invalidations are to release us from the guilt. Repent of the guilt and validation will flow.

- The glory of God has nothing to do with your faith level, opinions, thoughts, failures or your perceptions, but these things will keep you from carrying His glory.

- The glory of God was, is and always will be, regardless of anything.

- The glory of God is the I AM of your life.

- It doesn't take any participation on our part for the glory to be the glory. But in order to carry the glory, you must make yourself available for wholeness.

- You cannot mess up the glory of God.

- We cannot change His glory. We cannot rearrange His glory. All we can do is carry His glory.

- The glory of God is ageless and flawless.

- Not only does the glory of God heal wounds, hurts and insecurities, it also seals them.

- God's glory heals us from the inside out.

- When you walk in the glory, you are already walking in eternity.

- The only thing that will remove revelation is your own thoughts.

- Revelation will turn questions into statements of truth.

- When you stop questioning God, this confirms your faith in a God you've never seen.

- The glory cloud of God can overshadow you, captivate you, illuminate you and deliver you.

- The glory of God will take you into the secret place where you are healed from the inside out.

- The glory comes to take that which has come to irritate, hinder, or destroy.

- As you acknowledge the glory, it brings you forth and you are no longer stuck.

- The glory forces you to deal with yourself.

- The glory of God arises on you every day to set you free from yourself and others.

- The glory of God delivers, regardless of your sin.

- Sanctification and purification can only come in the glory of God.

- The mantle of the glory is truthfulness, confidence, continually, always, constantly, evermore, perpetual, strength and victory.

- Everything is retroactive in the glory.

- The glory of God, which is the light of God, brings forth the life of God and the love of God.

- The glory of God cannot be contained. You cannot put boundaries or limits on the glory of God.

- Under the glory, you will always have an answer.

- The glory of God teaches you how to have peace, joy and pleasure with yourself.

- The only qualification to carry the glory is to be made whole.

- The greater glory takes you into the supernatural.

- The glory of God will transport you to your destiny.

- The glory of God will reveal mysteries that have been hidden for generations.

- Good things happen under the glory of God.

- The glory will introduce you to God as the I AM.

- You either operate under your glory or His glory. You must look at the will to know the inheritance: my will be done or His will be done.

- Under revelation, you repent for your own opinions.

- The glory of God supersedes man's will only when acknowledged.

- When the glory makes you whole, it reveals your eternal identity and your old natural man becomes unfamiliar.

- The glory of God makes you new.

- The things that you frequently think of and don't let anyone know, are the revelation and glory of God. The opposite of this is your letting others always know your own thoughts.

- Revelation takes you out of a place in which you have been stuck and into a place where you can flow.

- Revelation empowers you to go beyond what the natural says and on into the supernatural.

- You disqualify yourself for revelation when you speak against yourself, because God's revelation brought you forth to shine.

- Excellence is the platform for God's glory.

- Under the glory of God, you see intentions.

- The glory of God exposes you, expands you and makes you transparent.

- The glory of God will bring forth His power.

- The glory of God wants to cauterize the phantom pains of our past problems.

- The amount of the glory on your life has to do with how you feel about yourself.

- Revelation brings clarity, peace, and completion.

- Confirmation will always escort revelation.

- God's revelation is on the other side of your dread.

- Revelation is an answer to impossible situations.

- Renovation turns into restoration by way of revelation.

- We must reserve a place within us where the glory of God can reside.

- God's glory will always come to bring forth His provisions.

- Under revelation, you operate with excellence and not assumptions.

- The glory and revelation of God will not only expose curses, but will also explain to you why they came.

- The glory and revelation of God will allow you to hear other people's thoughts.

- Under the glory, you have x-ray vision that enables you to see through deceptions.

- The glory brings forth an illumination that exposes divinations.

- The glory will attract you to transparency.

- Not only will the glory draw you to the truth, it will deliver you where you can become transparent.

-

- The glory of God illuminates, intensifies and magnifies.

- Under the glory you abide in the revelatory realm, which is right here and right now.

- The glory is the only thing that can take away the power of pain.

- When we get to the point that we can say our wills are finished, it's only then can the glory of God take us into the glory realm.

- The glory realm is the realm of heaven.

- The glory eliminates all deceptions.

- The glory of God changes you to the point that you don't recognize yourself.

- When you put yourself in the atmospheric pressure of His glory, it causes your life to be rearranged.

- The glory is a place of completion, and it is not as far away as you think.

- As the glory of God arises on you, it draws you to a place that you are destined to be.

- The lack of discernment can abort the impregnation of His glory.

- Revelation is indication that you have been intimate with God.

- Under the revelatory realm, everything has a reason. Coincidence cannot interrupt the revelatory realm; it has no authority.

True and False Intimacy

- False intimacy has nothing in common with anyone.

- We have built a false relationship with ourselves out of our brokenness.

- Intimacy is God meeting you right where you are.

- False intimacy is when you don't love and treat yourself as God does.

- True intimacy gets you in a rhythm with God's heartbeat.

- True Intimacy heals insecurities.

- Truth opens the door for insecurities to leave.

- True Intimacy exposes you and brings forth deliverance.

- A curse will always manifest as broken in the same manner that it comes to destroy.

- Disobedience can re-open a generational curse that has been broken.

- You have to lose every false, intimate relationship in order to be made whole.

- The prostitute that the Pharisees brought to Jesus (to be stoned) finally understood true intimacy, while the Pharisees fled in false intimacy.

- False intimacy will always bring intimidation.

- True intimacy is where revelation resides.

- We cover our brokenness up with false intimacy and call it Godliness.

- True intimacy intoxicates fear.

- False intimacy owns guilt and shame.

- Condemnation is conceived from false intimacy.

- What you have questioned your whole life can be answered by true intimacy.

- True intimacy is when you can love and be loved.

- Truth strengthens, liberates and exposes lies.

- True intimacy demands participation to be effective.

- Anytime you have a broken relationship, it's because you need to forgive.

- When you have a relationship with God, you don't need religion.

- True intimacy is fresh every morning.

- True intimacy will always introduce trust.

- Religion is the foundation of false intimacy.

- False intimacy is the counterfeit to true intimacy.

- False intimacy is supported by deceptions.

- True intimacy brings forth the manifestation of God's glory.

- True intimacy desires honesty.

- True intimacy instructs; false intimacy destructs.

- True intimacy doesn't take reasoning, just faith.

- False intimacy put Adam and Eve out of the garden.

- True intimacy doesn't bring up the past.

- When you're empty, it's all about you. When you're full, it's all about others.

- False intimacy will steal your true identity.

- False intimacy will bring forth confusion.

- False intimacy is escorted by false accusations.

- False intimacy is when you compare yourself to someone else.

- False intimacy is misery in an emotion.

- False intimacy always thinks that it is right, and everyone else is wrong.

- False intimacy is where condemnation is built.

- False intimacy interrupts wisdom.

- False intimacy makes you try to prove yourself.

- False intimacy has no life; it fades away.

- False intimacy creates a trust issue.

- When false intimacy is a part of your life, you associate yourself with failure.

- If we make ourselves available for true intimacy, it changes our atmosphere.

- When you have true intimacy, you get a download of spiritual information for deliverance.

- The day that you make the decision to get over yourself will be the introduction to true intimacy.

- We tear ourselves down when God is trying to build us up, and we call this relationship, but it is really dysfunction.

- A child that is raised without intimacy usually turns out to be an adult without discernment.

- Intimacy always brings understanding. When things are explained to an individual, it will cause an automatic acceleration of intellect.

- Intimacy is the evidence of His presence.

- Love is an explanation, not intimidation.

- When intimacy hasn't been taught, secrecy has been sought.

- The world knows intimidation, which is satan's counterfeit of intimacy.

- Commitment opens you up to the avenues of intimacy.

- Operating under invalidation is intimidation. Operating under validation brings forth intimacy.

- Love looks past faults.

- True intimacy offers in-depth explanations.

- True love never threatens.

- False intimacy will leave you bitter, angry and resentful.

- If you see things in others that aggravate and irritate you, it is only because you have it yourself.

- False intimacy destroys relationships.

- The counterfeit will always test your authority.

- As long as there is intimidation, there is no room for intimacy.

- Intimacy is the only thing that brings forth God's glory.

- Emptiness is the evidence of not being available for intimacy.

- Double-mindedness is looking in the mirror and not being able to see yourself as God sees you, therefore creating a false intimate relationship with yourself.

- False intimacy is when we don't see like God sees.

- Light (true intimacy) validates. Darkness (false intimacy) invalidates.

- Jealousy is the evidence of invalidation (false intimacy).

- True intimacy is the only avenue for validation.

- Validation brings wholeness.

- We must allow true intimacy to form validations within us and remove all residues from past invalidations that formed a false foundation.

- Rituals, traditions and routines will escort you to the place of desertion, known as false intimacy.

- False intimacy is the proud father of twins: fear and failure.

- False intimacy rejects any form of corrective criticism and claims it as judgment.

- When you are healed and made whole, corrective criticism will catapult you into your destiny.

- Feelings of unworthiness come as evidence of invalidations.

- Validation brings obedience, and obedience brings blessings.

- Validations void and cancel all invalidations.

- True intimacy heals.

- False intimacy destroys.

- True intimacy teaches you simplicity.

- False intimacy teaches you complication.

- Obstacles are anything that interrupts intimacy.

- False intimacy learns how to go around things and settle them with justification, instead of going through them.

- False intimacy will cause one to evacuate with no explanation.

- True trust is exercising true intimacy.

- Always expecting others to hurt you is based in false intimacy.

- True intimacy always brings forth impregnation.

- True intimacy doesn't need an introduction.

- True intimacy allows you to be who you are.

- False intimacy will always want you to be someone you are not.

- True intimacy has the power to make mere words a promise.

- Love is the ultimate action of true intimacy.

- False intimacy doesn't bring forth anything but miscarriages, abortions and death.

- True intimacy always impregnates you with understanding.

Time

- Time submits to patience.

- There is no time or distance in the glory.

- Prophecy encourages you to conform to Him.

- Before you see a miracle, you will always see wisdom. Miracles are the effect of Wisdom.

- The spirit of Elijah can take us us from where we are to where we need to be.

- Praise brings forth His presence. Worship brings forth His glory.

- Deception over time produces delusion.

- Faith is not an event, it's a lifestyle.

- Time was created when sin had to be accounted for.

- A word given out of season (a certain time) brings destruction.

- You have to know where you are, before you know where you're going.

- Time succumbs to brokenness.

- Prophetic words need time for confirmation, revelation confirms itself in now form.

- Hesitation is the counterfeit to expectation.

- Expectation is man having knowledge of the natural, choosing intimacy with God, thus producing an atmosphere of the supernatural, which brings forth miracles.

- The only thing that destroys expectation is regret.

- What you invest your time in, you will become.

- When traumas happen, they slow down time because they were never supposed to happen. Traumas have to insert themselves into time. Have you ever experienced something that seemed as if it was in slow motion?

- True prophetic won't sit around and wait for apologies.

- Prophetic process comes to pass when the old is renewed and the past is removed.

- A word out of season will destroy a man, be careful what you hear.

- Time brings forth purpose.

- Time represents inserts of eternity.

- Time is the enemy to eternity, there is no time in heaven, only eternity.

- One doesn't realize the value of a thing, until one lives without value.

- Today is your yesterday, tomorrow is your eternity.

- God doesn't want a visitation, He wants a habitation.

- Eternity is an expression of God's glory.

- You can't be satisfied today on a yesterday word.

- There has to be a place of insertion to bring the supernatural to the natural.

- Time is not measured in eternity.

- The difference in the past and the present is the manifestation of change.

- If you are not changing, you are still connected to your past.

- Your past has the power to keep you stuck in time.

- Time is a product of eternity.

- Release your past and the glory of God will catapult you into His time, which is destiny.

- If you are willing to change and have not, it's because you have fear of your past.

- Today's faith is eternity activated for now.

- Some try to operate in yesterday's faith for tomorrow and it brings confusion.

- Eternal atmospheric intimacy is when you can bring your problem and it will be wiped away, and not even have to be addressed.

- There is no seed time under the glory, only harvest.

- You are always only a day away from your destiny.

- Time will prove the truth to be true.

- The pains of our past will keep us in bondage of regret, unforgiveness and resentment.

- Your past can't compliment your future; so therefore, you must release it.

- Your past has the power to complicate and confuse your present.

- We can't carry the glory of God and our past at the same time.

- Our brokenness allows our past to have power over our future.

- There is no place for your past in the present.

- If you give your past a position in your present, then it has the power to interrupt your future.

- We release our past one pain at a time, and by repenting of the way that we tried to control our lives, to the point of almost destroying ourselves.

- Time as we know it is opposite to eternity, simply because time is limited and eternity is not limited.

- When eternal promises come forth, time as we know it has to bow in reverence to eternity, because it is the greater power.

- We are to analyze our past not sympathize with our past. If we sympathize with our past we begin to have self-pity for ourselves. If we analyze our past then we get to the bottom of the problem and find answers.

- What we are prepared for, we can overcome.

- Time is not demanding when you are in the secret place with God.

- Time is the only qualification to be intimate.

- In time, trust brings peace.

- Patience confirms a matter, impatience destroys a matter.

- Time will always confirm if it's God's revelation or satan's deception.

- Shame over time turns into guilt.

- If you do not dismiss yesterday, you cannot receive what God has for you today.

- When the supernatural and the natural collide, it is the deep calling the deep.

- You cannot predict your life with assumptions.

- If you are in balance and have peace, it is hard for traumas to find a way to be inserted into time.

Brokenness and Wholeness

- If you are broken, you can't project His glory, it will only be a shattered image.

- Brokenness is anything that keeps you from God.

- Trade in your place of brokenness when you have been dismantled, so God can mantle you with His wholeness (which is His glory).

- The mantle of brokenness is the yoke of heaviness and the mantle of wholeness is His yoke that is LIGHT.

- Brokenness produces time without a purpose. Wholeness is purpose that compliments time.

- What is not made whole, projects brokenness.

- You have got to be aware of your surroundings to be made whole.

- Wholeness is the opposite of Brokenness.

- The more whole you become, the more you prosper. If you are not prospering it is because you can't contain what He is pouring out upon you.

- It is easier to hold onto your brokenness than to be accountable to your wholeness.

- Being whole takes faith, being broken takes fear.

- We agree too easily with brokenness, while resisting wholeness.

- You can't be sanctified and broke inside.

- The degree of your brokenness is determined by what you hide inside.

- We have operated in false intimacy so long that we can't seem to find wisdom.

- False intimacy has interrupted our relationship with wisdom.

- Trying to be something that you are not is evidence of false intimacy.

- The way to become holy is to become whole.

- The way to become holy is to make yourself available to wholeness.

- When you are made whole, you no longer tolerate brokenness.

- When your inner self awakens and comes alive, nothing can shut you down.

- Your brokenness will manipulate others, to get its way.

- Brokenness makes one very selfish.

- Wholeness heals brokenness.

- Evidence of your wholeness is when you no longer question Him.

- Evidence of your brokenness is when your doubt and discouragement drive you to question His motives.

- Our brokenness produces self-pity and pity of others.

- Sympathy is a dressed up word for pity.

- Brokenness is the evidence of sin.

- Brokenness desires brokenness to be satisfied.

- Wholeness is when we allow pleasure to overcome our pain.

- What we don't allow God to uncover will become a veil that we will hide behind.

- Invalidations will leave holes in your life that you will always try to fill.

- Brokenness takes dominion over authority only when given permission.

- Authority brings domain.

- Righteous authority brings companionship.

- You must be aware of your surroundings to be made whole.

- Our wholeness has to be greater than our brokenness.

- Our minds have to be greater than our past painful experiences.

- Double-mindedness is a curse that causes you to look in the mirror with disgust.

- Disgust turns to bitterness if not repented of.

- When others hurt us, it is because of their brokenness. They usually think that their pain is greater than yours, but in all actuality, yours is greater because you just took some of theirs.

- Order is evidence of your wholeness. Disorder is evidence of brokenness.

- Order brings forth stages, phases and levels. Disorder tears down and brings forth ruins.

- The deeper that we let fear, doubt and unbelief reside within us will be the evidence of our brokenness.

- Deliverance comes when we decide to change.

- When you don't speak with a renewed mind, you have the power to interrupt others.

- Busyness is a form of drivenness. Busyness is brokenness being revealed.

- You find validation in being busy but you don't have to be busy to find yourself.

- You can't minster to someone out of your own brokenness because you will end up feeling sorry for them.

- If you can't love yourself, you are behind bars of self-bitterness and self-judgment.

- Don't tolerate what you have been accumulating, that causes confusion.

- Toleration aborts acceleration.

- Negative emotions set you up for a shut down in the physical.

- When you conquer your mind and thoughts, then you can conquer your body.

- When I understand my imperfections and stop judging myself and others, then I will be on neutral ground.

- What you don't judge you will receive knowledge from.

- Wholeness does not tolerate brokenness when found out.

- God can't set us free when we tolerate brokenness. Brokenness keeps us where we cannot display His power.

- Emptiness is attracted to wholeness, this is why it is important for us to be made whole. When someone is made whole their very presence heals.

- According to your brokenness will be the way that you analyze your own thoughts and others.

- You cannot trust a Holy God with a half heart.

- You cannot love wholly with holes in your heart.

- I made myself sick from being sick of myself.

- We hear the enemy out of our brokenness, but we hear God out of our wholeness.

- The degree that you hear the Lord is the evidence of your wholeness.

- Wholeness is royalty.
  Your Highness/Your Wholeness

- Brokenness will talk all the time; wholeness will be still and hear.

- We were not created for comparison, we were created for completeness.

- The broken places in our lives are the hidden places we keep from God.

- The places that we hide will never be healed.

- Painful perceptions are formed out of our brokenness.

- If you don't have balance, you do not have power. Imbalances are evidence of brokenness.

- When you try to fix someone else you operate in idolatry.

- We try to fix others only because we can't seem to be able to do anything with ourselves.

- Your fear empowers assumptions that have been assumed from your brokenness.

Anger, Bitterness and Judgments

- Anger is judgment towards yourself and others.

- Anything that aggravates or irritates you stems from judgments.

- Judgments bring forth curses.

- Our minds try to hold us in judgment with our past experiences.

- We end up in a place of bondage because that's where we've judged ourself to be.

- Pride will cause you to be prejudiced.

- What you don't overcome, will overcome you.

- Seclusion doesn't teach you anything but loneliness.

- Bitterness and self bitterness is saying, "God allowed it."

- When you hold things back, you are poisoning yourself.

- The places of incompletion keep you in disabilities.

- When your heart becomes hard, that's when your body breaks.

- Gossip is fueled by accusations which are established by judgments.

- Any form of bitterness hinders the way in which we hear God.

- Self-bitterness, self-hatred and self-judgment are all negative emotions that will cause afflictions and will allow an unloving spirit to operate in your life.

- Negative emotions cause judgments.

- By judging yourself, you cause a curse to come upon your life of bitterness, hatred and judgment, which causes loneliness.

- We have sympathized with ourselves in our bitterness and blamed it on others, and that in return has kept us in bondage to our fear of failures.

- When you are busy judging others, you forget to repent.

- Things that offend you are because you are trying to defend your brokenness.

Truth and Deception

- When we don't rightly discern deception, we try to find comfort in calling it God's will.

- If we would love as much as we judge, then our judgment could turn into discernment.

- Our discernment brings healing.

- Confusion is the seed to a harvest of chaos.

- Lack of deliverance also brings an abundance of chaos.

- Our judgment brings death.

- Deceptions invite the counterfeits.

- Failure to man is destruction. Failure to God is something without form.

- Deception is the counterfeit which creates an atmosphere of common accusations and opinions; whereas Revelation creates an atmosphere of truth to change what has been to what is about to be.

- Anything that ends up empty was formed out of a foundation of deception.

- A foundation of truth will always bring forth abundance.

- The counterfeit will always come right before the real thing.

- Man's opinion is not God's revelation.

- You don't have to carry the call when God calls you. You are the call!

- Perversion is anything that is not God's version.

- If you knew how much power is in your words, you would choose them more truthfully.

- Contentment is the counterfeit to peace.

- Things are not always as though they seem.

- Justification will keep you in bondage.

- Justification is not deliverance.

- Justification is the procrastination of your deliverance.

- God wants your wrong decisions to be assets to take you through your deliverance.

- Self-pity seclusion doesn't teach you anything but loneliness.

- We are called to be more than we have condemned ourselves to be.

- Relationships don't take reasoning, they take faith.

- Relationship is determined by trust.

- Condemnation keeps you from hearing and seeing what God is trying to give to you as a gift.

- Sin is not accepting yourself for the way He created you to be.

- Blasphemy is knowing that you could be healed and not seeking it.

- You can't think palace when you're in poverty.

- You will never understand the palace place as long as you are stuck in poverty.

- My faith gives me peace, not my surroundings. If I allow my faith to come forth, then my surroundings have to line up with His peace.

- We have agreed with deception for so long and called it peace, that we don't recognize the SHALOM of God.

- The shalom of God is nothing missing, nothing broken.

- Your faith, peace and discernment will cause satanic forces to manifest.

- Discernment finds the truth as it searches for it, but judgment only justifies deception.

- Where there is unity, there is power.

- Symptoms of affliction are satanic projections of deception.

- When we get in the way of God by trying to do things ourselves, that's occultism.

- Deception will always leave you doubting.

- Obedience occupies patience.

- Deception will allow you to justify evil.

- Deception brings misery.

- The enemy operates under magnification.

- God operates out of multiplication.

- Truth demands acknowledgment and authority. Authority produces respect.

- When you acknowledge the truth, it always makes a way.

- Truth always brings change.

Order of intellect:
Knowledge
Understanding
Wisdom

- Assumption is bred from deception.

- Inferiority is the counterfeit to authority.

- Counterfeits will always try to keep you from the truth.

- When we allow untruths to form wrong perceptions within us, this allows fear, doubt and unbelief to have authority over us.

- Perception is the foundation that deceptions are built upon.

- Truth requires concentration to bring forth completeness.

- As the truth penetrates you, it sets you free.

- Anything other than the truth is deception and deception is death.

- Truth opens the door to all insecurities, to let them all out.

- Acknowledge your mistakes and file them in a category of your past in order to enter into your destiny.

- To have life, you must have the truth to set you free so that you can find the way.

- If you can't treat yourself good then you automatically give others permission to treat you that way.

- Hurt People-Hurt People.

- Discern what it is that attracts you to people. Is it their brokenness or wholeness? Is it your brokenness or wholeness?

- Confusion comes when we try to make things work according to our own understanding.

- We have complicated our lives to the point that simplicity seems foreign.

- The only power that your past has over you is the power that you give it permission to have.

- Faith produces love and love always travels with peace.

- Anything that is counterfeit will fail because it is built out of pride.

- Unbelief keeps you out of your destiny.

- Love is known as a life-giving source of power.

- If it is truth, it won't be offended. If it is a lie, it needs to be offended.

- Discernment disqualifies darkness as power.

- Evil cannot reveal evil, only truth reveals evil.

- When you analyze your past, you get set free. When you sympathize with your past you stay in bondage to it.

- It's only an idea when it is thought about, but when it takes root, it becomes truth. Don't let your ideas uproot truth.

- Deception will keep you from operating under mercy and truth.

- If you walk with Mercy and Truth on your life, this will keep you from a premature death. This is a promise that your children and grandchildren will inherit.

- The evidence of what the enemy does is according to the amount of authority that you operate in.

- The majority of our wholeness is determined by our willingness to destroy denial.

- The lack of comprehension will encourage the attitude of complaint.

- The lack of discernment creates false prophecies.

- Real is first cousin to truth.

- Pride causes aggression, humility causes progression.

- If you have to hold onto something, then you don't really have anything. Let it go and if it's yours, it will return.

- You have to conceive it before you can believe it.

- A prisoner isn't free if he gets out for visitation.

- Pastors are supposed to lead a flock, not feed a flock. You're on your own when it comes to eating.

- Discernment is the device that counteracts the weapons that have already been formed against you.

- Being comfortable is the counterfeit peace. Peace goes beyond comfort.

- Discernment is received in solitude. The enemy would try to make you think that solitude is loneliness.

- Discernment is knowing the difference between good and evil. Mature discernment is choosing the good.

- Discernment brings light to darkness, clarity to confusion and resolve to problems.

- Instruction that is not discerned sets you up for rebellion.

- Corrective criticism when discerned catapults you to purpose.

- Truth is your friend. Deception is your enemy.

- Truth has to be accepted before it can bring change.

- The hardest thing about change is acknowledging that you need it.

- Truth has a harder time getting our attention than distractions.

- There is a big difference between authority and allowance. You have to define the two.

- The wilderness is one step away from the garden.

- You are always one step away from your destiny. Don't give up!

- The only thing that will take you out of the garden is negative emotions.

- Our assumptions are not God's intentions.

- If your body is sick, it is because your soul has remained wounded.

- Unworthiness will decapitate your authority as entertainment.

- Truth is known by the spirit that is within us. Deception has to be discerned in the natural.

- Discernment comes from being intimate with God.

- False intimacy breeds misunderstanding, chaos, confusion, division, retaliation, divorce, destruction and devastation which are all precursors to the death of a relationship.

- Faith is something that you know is coming. Fear is what tries to stop it from arriving.

- Faith expands the portal to the supernatural.

- If the enemy can get you to tear yourself down, you won't be a threat to his darkness.

- Stubbornness is pride.

- Humility is the first step to being healed.

- If you have unanswered questions, you have believed a lie.

- People that keep up with the JONES' are not only high maintenance, but they need high deliverance.

- Sometimes we stretch ourselves too thin and call it God, it's a false pregnancy and you give birth to bitterness and still try to call it God.

- You have to experience failure before you can know victory.

- We maintain dysfunction which is deception and call it LIFE.

- To prove a point is deception and manipulation.

- Thoughts are heavy and bring confusion. Knowledge is light and brings peace.

- Desolation is when man's ideas turn into ashes.

- The difference between an idea and truth is the root.

- The evidence of what the enemy does is according to your authority.

- The lack of comprehension will encourage the spirit of complaining.

- The lack of discernment creates false prophets.

- The more information you have, the more authority you have, because authority is power.

- Pride causes aggression, humility causes progression.

- Believe nothing is impossible and then you become unlimited.

- When truth is questioned it should not bring offense. However, deception will always bring defense.

- Things and people die prematurely because of repetition, when we should desire revelation over repetition.

- A generational curse is any repetitious pattern of destruction.

- Revelation comes to break the law of repetition.

- Revelation has no part of repetition, because it is truth.

- Truth proves to be true but deception has to repeat itself by repetition to convince one that it is true.

- The very thing you think that you have figured out, you will only be on the back side of it.

- The thing that you say that you don't have, will be the very thing that you do have.

- Simplicity is the key to prosperity.

- When you have balance, peace comes. Imbalance and turmoil come with distress.

- Line up with God and your faith will know that everything is possible.

- Your despair can turn into your destiny if you will turn to God.

- Unconscious accusations against God are when you think God caused bad things to happen.

- As long as you blame God, things will get worse for you because of the judgment you have against God.

- Things that look impossible are only opportunities to be acknowledged as possible.

- Knowledge is the platform for wisdom.

- You have to operate in knowledge before God can reveal His wisdom.

- Discernment disables weapons that have already been formed against you.

- Best is the enemy to excellence.

- Bitterness will always dethrone you from royalty.
- Royalty is when you carry His glory.

- The information that remains in you and has yet to be discerned remains as ignorance.

- Honor yourself so your children will honor you.

- Feelings of unworthiness keep us imprisoned to poverty.

- Despair that denies Him and partners with darkness, births destruction.

- Expectations always bring forth manifestations.

- Discernment disables destruction.

- You can't give what you don't have.

- Peace is not present when unanswered questions remain.

- You have to know where you are to know where you are going.

- Immaturity is evidence of brokenness that will keep you entrapped to hopelessness.

- The very thing that you won't deal with now will deal with you later and derail you from God's promises.

- If you don't stand for the truth, you will fall for anything.

- When you pity others, you set yourself up for a failure.

- If your house doesn't have order, then your life doesn't have order.

- If your heart is broken, chances are that your trust is broken too.

- It takes a whole heart to trust wholly.

- In the secret place with God, you have to deal with yourself.

- Everything that has been concealed will be revealed in the secret place.

- Confirmation will always be heard in the secret place with God.

- Bad things happen to good people, not because God allows them to!

- Bad things happen to good people because of evil!

- Sympathy is different than compassion.

- Sympathy allows symptoms the right to remain.

- Sympathy is formed from self-pity.

- Truth remains when deception drains.

- If you are not straight with God then you become crooked with man.

- Trust is deeper than faith, you must become vulnerable.

Submission

- Submission to God is permission to pour out His Wisdom, that teaches you how to resist the enemy.

- When we oppose submission we resist the Wisdom of God, when we are supposed to be resisting the devil, by way of submission.

- We resist submission and remove restitution. Restitution comes when we resist the enemy. We have been resisting the wrong thing!

- When you submit yourselves one to another, your insecurities have to flee.

- What you don't admit to, you submit to.

- Allow yourself to be stretched out over a Holy God and everything you thought that would overcome you, you will overcome it.

- Submission is stretching.

- Anytime we have to prove ourselves, God isn't getting His way, we are in the way.

- Your position with God is based on the people that you give honor to.

- You operate in faith when you fully surrender your fear.

- Confirmation brings confidence.

- Confirmation is courage that turns into encouragement.

- What you create, you have to correct.

- The greater your battle, the greater your victory.

- Wickedness is anything that you disagree with God about.

- When truth is questioned it shouldn't bring offense. What brings offense is the deception that is already within us.

- Deception needs to be questioned and exposed.

- If you have a hard time trusting others and yourself, then you are fooling yourself that you are trusting God.

- Discernment doesn't need your concern, only your availability to hear the truth.

- Personal concern aborts discernment.

- If you have more than three broken relationships in your life right now, you need to change.

- Submit to confirmation and reject competition.

Obedience and Disobedience

- Obedience to Him brings you to a spontaneous meltdown, which is the evidence of change occurring.

- Disobedience can re-open a generational curse that has been broken.

- Time obeys obedience.

- When we are obedient to God, He inserts divine appointments and opportunities into our time.

- When you are obedient even in the midst of your own pain, the evil that has come against you will turn on itself.

- When God calls you to be obedient and destroys negative things in your life and you choose to procrastinate, then the negative things end up destroying you.

- Carrying the glory of God is evidence of being made whole.

- The difference in being called or chosen is obedience.

- Offerings have the opportunity to adjust your child's inheritance.

- Obedience brings prosperity.

- Take time to bless, to break the curse.

- Obedience brings impregnation. Resistance and rebellion bring forth abortions.

- Justification will keep you away from glorification.

- Obedience brings forth authority.

- The reason others won't listen to you is because you don't listen to yourself.

- Obedience brings clarity, disobedience brings confusion.

- Destruction comes shortly after confusion.

- Repentance of disobedience clears up the cloud of confusion so the cloud of God's glory can reside.

- The cloud of confusion is the counterfeit to the cloud of God's glory.

- Clarity erases confusion.

- When you are obedient in the Spirit it brings forth wholeness in the natural.

- You can be broken on the inside but successful on the outside.

- Rebellion and disobedience throw us into a fourth generation of curses.

- Faith does not need associations or assumptions.

- The enemy tries to mock God by encouraging your presumptions.

- Curses come when you are disobedient to your purpose.

Blessings and Curses

- Generational Curses will always manifest themselves in the same manner in which they come to destroy.

- Disobedience births destructions that can lead to curses.

- Double-mindedness is a generational curse that you were taught.

- Double-mindedness is looking in the mirror and refusing to see yourself as you are.

- Fear brings forth curses.

- Faith brings forth blessings.

- When you judge something, you put it under a curse which puts you under a curse.

- Generational Curses can be broken under the glory of God.

- When knowledge and obedience get together, then wisdom can build a foundation for true intimacy.

- Rebellion is a curse from our forefathers that hold us in captivity.

- Generational curses if not broken, become greater.

- A generational curse that conceals itself for several generations gains power.

- A generational curse that is procrastinated will be become more powerful.

- The only way that a generational curse can come on you is if you procrastinate your deliverance. Procrastinating opens a legal door of access for the enemy.

- Generational curses can interrupt great faith.

- When a generational curse is broken, the pain has to stop and pleasure has to take its rightful position.

- Pride pushes and seeks approval.

- Disobedience and rebellion bring curses.

- Curses that are ignored are empowered.

- Procrastination will allow a curse to remain and operate as active in your life.

- Acknowledging a curse as broken will accelerate the manifestation of the curse to be broken.

- Confirmation of a curse is its power that it has over you.

- In order to be free from a curse you must get out from under it by way of being obedient to God.

- Fear will allow a generational curse to manifest and steal from you what really belongs to you.

- Curses always have traumatic intentions and malicious motives.

- In order to break a curse you must first seek and find the cause of the curse. Whatever caused the curse, repent of the cause that has affected your life and family.

- Make a decision to quit living under the influence of the effects and break the cause of the curse.

- The more curses that we break over our lives, the longer we will live on this earth.

- Breaking curses today is leaving an inheritance to your children and your grandchildren.

- If you don't break a curse, you will enable it.

- Complication is evidence of a curse.

- Blessings counteract curses.

- Generational curses skip a generation to conceal themselves to gain more power.

- If you have everything a person would need or desire and you're still not happy, you may be under a generational curse.

- Curses come from the forefather's loins and the mother's wombs (Exo. 34:7, Ps. 51:5).

- If you can't identify a curse, then you're stuck with it.

- Why do I do the things that I shouldn't and not get done the things that I should be doing? Can we say curse?

- Generational curses come to make you think that they are part of you.

- When you think that everybody else is your problem, you're "not loving yourself" is the only problem.

- Curses can only compliment brokenness.

- If you won't hear the Spirit of God by putting the curse to rest, then you run the risk of it putting you to rest.

Why do we wait until we die to rest in peace?

- Usually generational curses manifest when you have judged someone harshly in your family.

**The curses that we don't break today,
our children may succumb to tomorrow.**

- If you're not operating in love, you are operating under a curse.

- Intimacy breaks curses.

- True intimacy dissolves generational curses.

- When you seek out a curse, it will manifest!

- Curses that are ignored, GROW.

- The only justification of curses is the person ignoring it.

- Some people call them fits, I call it a curse manifesting.

- Emptiness is the effect of a curse.

- Curses allow unanswered questions to remain.

- When God blesses something it is to be from everlasting to everlasting.

- When curses are broken, blessings can manifest.

- Things that you can't seem to shake are usually because they are deep rooted by a curse. Ask God to reveal the curse.

- Automatic curses are birthed from the lack of knowledge, accusations and judgment.

- Emptiness is the evidence of busyness.

- The only difference in emptiness and overflow is obedience.

- Opinions and accusations allow curses to remain.

- Truth and obedience disintegrate darkness.

- Traumas are demonic doors that open you up to curses.

- As long as you try to be comfortable, that compliments curses.

- If you seek comfort then you pacify a curse.

- Comfort is not peace.

- Breaking curses will keep you from the storms of tribulation.

- Repentance brings restoration to things that have been cursed.

- When a curse hits a curse, it has to identify itself.

Pain, Distress and Despair

- Despair does not have to be your enemy. Despair births a desire within you to choose Him.

- Pain is addictive. It wants you to think that you can't live without it.

- Despair that is yoked up to darkness brings destruction.

- Despair that is yoked up with truth brings breakthrough.

- Your despair will drive you to find the mysteries of God.

- We are people of association. Our pains and past experiences have left a residue within us that encourages us to associate the past with our present.

- You have to be desperate before a desire can be birthed within you to seek His will over your own.

- Despair that seeks His light, will bring life.

- If you think that God does things for other people but can't do it for you, then you are serving the god of self-pity.

- Self- pity will remove you from the glory.

- When you find your wholeness, then pain has to apologize to your body as it flees.

- Your despair can birth a desire to see your destiny.

- Hardships produce hardness.

- The pains of hardships become part of us, if not repented of.

- Guilt and shame will turn your head away from the truth.

- Despair will drive you to seek out the hidden mysteries of God.

- Pain has to be identified.

- Pain that is not identified and repented of has the spiritual legal right to manifest.

- In the midst of pain there is no neutral ground. You either go up or down.

- If you allow it to, your pain can catapult you into your destiny.

- We've been so hurt by people that we won't let them in. We don't make room for people because we don't know compassion.

- Compassion takes you to an intimacy with God to understand His power. If you want to walk in signs, wonders and miracles, you have to learn compassion over your pain.

- If faith has taken us this far, what can compassion do? How much more will it accelerate us to the glory realm?

- Compassion will catapult you to the areas that God has for you to be complete.

- When His compassion comes, it sets us free from any counterfeit.

- Trade in your pain for His peace and you will always get to your destination.

- Don't miss your purpose because of your pain.

- Once you get free from pain, you no longer tolerate it. Once you find the source and get yourself healed emotionally, if the pain tries to return you learn to reject it and not yourself.

- Self-judgment will block you from hearing God.

- Traumas cause us to stay stuck.

- If there is pain associated with a past memory then you haven't forgiven.

- Inflammation is the evidence of issues that have not been dealt with.

- We should be a nation full of revelation instead of inflammation.

- If you don't deal with the issue, you won't have authority over the pain.

- Pain only exists in time, not eternity.

- Is pain the problem or your perception of the problem?

- The things that have afflicted you are the things you have not attended to.

- The freedom that you desire for others, you should desire for yourself.

- Don't let your brokenness detour you from your destiny.

- People cannot hurt you, if you are not already hurt.

- If someone offends you, it is your fault. The wound was there to start with.

- We tend to blame God when promises don't come to pass. He's been waiting on us to call down His glory to bring change to us and then it changes our situations.

- Whatever takes authority over you is what you are in bondage to.

Forgiveness and Unforgiveness

- Judgments are forms of unforgiveness.

- If you have a pain with a past memory then you haven't forgiven.

- Forgiveness is forgetfulness.

- You disengage unforgiveness by repenting of judgment.

- Unforgiveness breeds rebellion and rebellion is witchcraft.

- Accusations are aggravated opinions.

- Forgiveness and repentance help you go up. Haughtiness and arrogance will take you down.

- It takes forgiveness to be a servant.

- Servanthood doesn't impress, it influences.

- Servanthood never seeks opinions, just opportunities.

Servanthood never expects anything in return.

- Servanthood just is.

- A servant is someone who serves without reservation or neglect.

- Don't get good deeds confused with servanthood. Good deeds will eventually birth bitterness.

- If I blame others, I will never repent of my own sin.

- You can't be free unless you forgive yourself.

- Unforgiveness in your heart keeps you from the wisdom of God.

- Unforgiveness will make you think things are one-sided.

- We place judgment on others when we have unforgiveness towards ourselves.

- You cannot forgive others until you first forgive yourself.

- Unforgiveness holds you from receiving your freedom.

- When forgiveness is activated, there is a paradigm shift that takes place, and suddenly you see yourself no longer as the victim but victorious.

- As long as you have unforgiveness in your heart you will be stuck in the pain of that past.

- Repentance and forgiveness are the answers to bring forth the kingdom of God to earth.

- Judgment slips in when you try to figure others out, bitterness slips in when you can't figure yourself out.

- When you try to figure people out, judgment begins to disfigure you.

Exposure, Addition, Expansion and Abundance

- Expansion is a direct result of a glory insertion, because you made room for Him, He made room for you.

- Exposure introduces you to expansion.

- Addiction is the counterfeit to addition.

- The glory of God will take you to the place of expansion.

- Expansion is evidence of you moving from glory to glory.

- Exposure takes you into a place of expansion, and this prepares you for abundance.

- Exposure makes you transparent.

- Pride will hinder you from provisions.

- Worldly prosperity isn't kingdom. Worldly prosperity has the ability to change you. Kingdom prosperity has the ability to change others through you.

- Just because you were made from dust (dirt), doesn't mean you should treat yourself like dirt.

- Impregnation empowers deliverance. We welcome impregnation but procrastinate our deliverance.

- You have to inquire to acquire.

- We have to endure exposure to be embraced.

- Exposure brings deliverance.

- Exposure takes you to the place of acceleration.

- Expansion comes when you are under the glory, spiritually, mentally and physically.

- Visions don't come to divide, visions come to provide.

- Trials and temptations are to be testified of and not lived under.

- Every thought you have has an original, righteous intention.

- Exposure is not supposed to bring judgment. Exposure is supposed to bring healing.

- Expansion will take you from where you have been stuck and catapult you to your destiny in the glory.

- When one has insecurities and failures, you want to hide, but you need to expose yourself so you can be made whole.

- Self-pity is the foundation of every addiction and affliction that has ever been.

- When you put faith in your affliction, that is darkness.

Rest, Repentance and Restoration

- Rest is the evidence of restoration.

- You judging yourself for not being able to change yourself has kept you from changing.

- There has to be repentance of self-judgment before the veil of self-judgment can be removed.

- Repentance opens the heavens to reign.

- Lack of Repentance causes a repetition and reputation of pain. I don't want to be notorious for my brokenness, but acknowledged for my wholeness.

- Restoration is not painful, it is powerful.

- Repentance will always bring reflection.

- Repentance will always bring healing to you and others regardless of the seemingly hopeless situation. Broken relationships can be salvaged.

- We must deal with the root of our situations and circumstances or the weeds of unrighteousness will continue to spring up.

- Repentance is the only place that you can see yourself as you really are.

- Repentance is the only thing that can break the ramifications of the judgments that have already been made.

- Fear not repented of turns into torment.

- Rest is the greatest weapon for spiritual warfare.

- It takes humility to repent.

- When you forgive but can't forget, this is a feeling and not a healing.

- In order to receive, you must rest.

- If you don't have rest, you don't have a nest for revelation.

- If you don't know what rest is in the supernatural, you will never find it in the natural.

- Reconciliation is produced by repentance.

- Mistakes manifest more mistakes unless repented of.

- Repentance always brings healing.

- God has a blessing in our atmosphere awaiting our repentance.

- True repentance disqualifies dread.

- Not being available for deliverance will detour you from your destiny.

- The freer you get, the more you see your purpose.

- The degree of what you are delivered from today will be the degree of favor that your children will have tomorrow.

- Change brings forth restoration.

- If you are willing to change, it will bring forth a manifestation of God.

- True repentance comes when you become sick of yourself.

- The strategy of God is REST.

- True repentance brings a paradigm shift.

- Repentance makes you available for revelation.

- Repentance always brings restoration.

- Repentance eradicates you and places you on neutral ground.

- Trade in your place of secrecy of shame and guilt for the secret place in Psalm 91.

- Anything that you want to keep as a secret is usually based in sin.

- When you are made whole, you quit trying to prove yourself.

- Restoration awaits our response to revelation.

- The things that we don't repent of will affect our children and grandchildren.

- Repentance introduces you to revelation and glory.

- The degree in which you hear the voice of God is determined by the amount of repentance.

- We must repent and replace our ignorance with knowledge, and stop the process of destruction.

- God is the only one that can heal us of our past anguishes and present torments, so there must be an exchange of apologies.

- True repentance is an apology to God.

- Daily repentance and forgiveness is a must in this process of being made whole for the glory of God.

- Repentance brings renovation and restoration that replaces the hardness of our hearts.

- If we have God's presence, we will have His rest.

- God's presence has to be invited and then you will become united with His peace.

- God's revelation leads you to a place of rest, and rest escorts you on into restoration.

- Rest is opening yourself up to restoration.

- It is in the place of wait that we see God more clearly and things change in the process of wait.

- Convenience is the platform for complaints.

- We need to adapt to the mentality of waiting because this is the place of renewal.

- Your availability to rest establishes a place, and your faith invites the glory to come, and as you wait in His presence, this is the place where miracles come forth.

- Desolation comes after restoration to take you into a place of visitation and on to your destination; desolation is not your destiny.

- Holiness is the end result of wholeness, which comes by way of repentance.

- Repentance is the answer to staying in the secret place with God.

- Repentance is the medium that heals the soul.

- Lack of repentance will allow decay to clothe you and give you the false thought to say that it is God.

The Anointing and The Glory

- The anointing took Jesus to the cross but the glory took Him from the cross.

- The glory takes you from the place in which you been stuck for years and moves you into a glorious place that is called your destiny.

- The anointing tells you how to do and the glory shows what to do.

- The anointing is the introduction to intimacy that brings forth His glory.

- The anointing prepares you for the glory.

- The glory introduces you to true intimacy.

- The glory will take you into a place of wholeness.

- The anointing directs you to the kingdom and the glory takes you there.

- The glory will come to take you into an intoxicating place of intimacy with Him.

- God's glory brings illumination. God's glory is illumination.

- Illumination cannot be interrupted by darkness.

- The anointing of God sustains you but the glory of God moves you from glory to glory.

- The anointing comes to set us free and take us to a place of dying to ourselves. The glory of God can then take us over ourselves.

- The glory of God will bring you victory over yourself and your circumstances.

- The glory will pull you out of the place in which you have been stuck.

- The glory of God brings habitation and revelation.

- The glory of God will let you hear the thoughts of others.

- Your sensitivity is sky-rocketed under the glory of God.

- When the glory is present, all things become possible.

- The glory is a convincing manifestation of His presence.

- The glory that is reflected in you exposes evil in others, so that they can be delivered.

- The anointing heals over time, the glory heals immediately.

- Casual is the counterfeit. Common is supernatural. Supernatural should be normal.

- The glory will not consume you but it will engulf you. The burning bush was engulfed, not consumed.

- If something consumes you, then it is the counterfeit to keep you from being engulfed by God's glory.

- If we breathe, move and have our being in Him, every move that we make under the glory of God is recorded in heaven.

- The glory has to have a nest to rest and reside in. If we don't make room for the glory to come and reside then we just get by.

- The glory will fill you up and set you free from the deepest, darkest places that no one knows about but God.

- The glory will cause you to deal with yourself.

- When the glory manifests in color, it is to bring change to little details of your life.

- The lesser glory is in the lights, the greater glory is in you!

- The glory will make you transparent. The glory also transfigures you from your brokenness.

- The glory will set you free from being stuck and catapult you to your destiny.

- When you come under the glory, then you possess the glory.

- The glory simplifies everything around you.

- The glory is alive.

- The Glory will force you to deal with yourself, even the areas that you despise.

- The glory of God brings mantles, if you don't stop with the gifts and the anointing, you will run into His glory.

- Have you ever thought that there was more than just carrying the gifts and the anointing? There is. It's the glory.

- The spirit of excellence will provide a platform for the glory to land upon.

- To see in, through and behold, is to be in the glory.

- To see in the natural is to look upon. To see in the spirit is to believe upon.

- Under the glory you are: Unstoppable, Limitless, Ageless and Fearless.

- Your fear and your faith have to collide in order for the glory to manifest.

- There is no warfare in the glory. The warfare is outside of the glory. If you are tired of warfare, then get into the glory realm.

- When you allow yourself to be bombarded by yourself, this is warfare.

- God's miracles and our mistakes have nothing in common.

- The heaviness of depression and oppression is the counterfeit to the Kabod of God. The Kabod of God is the weightiness of God. The glory of God is heavy!

- The anointing takes you to a place but the glory takes you from a place. It's a matter of going in or coming out.

- The glory will open doors that have been shut by our fears, doubts and unbeliefs.

- Under the glory the revelation of God finds you.

- The very thing in your life that you won't deal with, will be the very thing that disables you from carrying the glory of God.

- God orchestrates overflow, not emptiness.

- In order to see God face to face, we must first see ourselves as He sees us.

- Under the anointing, you are called. Under the glory you are chosen.

- Under the anointing you usually have a lot of unanswered questions. Under the glory revelation gives you the answers.

- Under the anointing you operate in the prophetic realm. Under the glory you operate in the revelatory realm.

- Under the anointing you can still be broken. Under the glory you are made whole.

- Being full of holes (broken) is the counterfeit to holiness.

- Wholeness is the first step to holiness.

- Under the anointing you put band-aids on your wounds. Under the glory you expose your wounds where God can heal them.

- The anointing heals from the outside in but the glory heals from inside out.

- The glory of God will take you to the secret place where you can see yourself as He does.

- Prophecy prepares you for the manifestation of revelation.

- Revelation is a word that is now coming to pass. Prophecy is a word that will come to pass.

- God has an anointing for you. Satan has an addiction for you.

- The anointing equips you but the glory transfers and transports you.

- A visitation from God's glory will drive you to your destiny.

- Sanctification comes when we are made whole and the next phase after being sanctified is to be glorified.

- When His glory comes forth, He reveals who you are to yourself.

- You cannot see the glory unless you are awakened from the slumber of the anointing.

- The disciples were anointed but yet fell asleep as Jesus was preparing in the garden to be glorified.

- When you are anointed you operate under the prophetic realm which needs time to unfold. Under the glory you operate under the revelatory realm which is right here and right now.

- Jesus is the anointed Son of God that had to step down out of the glory into time to fulfill prophecy and also show us an example of walking in a greater place which is the glory.

- Jesus said, "Greater works than these we will do" (he was talking about us walking in the glory).

- Jesus was dismantled from the anointing so that the glory could take Him back to eternity.

- We must be available to be dismantled ourselves from the things that have kept us from carrying the glory.

- You have to be unveiled to be reveiled with the glory.

- The cloud of confusion is the counterfeit to the cloud of His glory.

Understanding and Misunderstanding

- If you don't understand something it is because you are standing under misunderstanding. Whatever is over you has authority over you.

- If the lack of understanding causes destruction, then understanding causes promotion.

- If you don't understand something you need to be willing to change positions and seek understanding.

- Understanding comes when sought.

- The closer you get to the throne, the more the enemy's voice sounds like His own.

- Understanding His glory brings power, misunderstanding of His glory brings emptiness.

- Knowledge takes understanding to form wisdom.

- Knowledge has to be united with understanding to receive wisdom.

- If you hear knowledge and do not understand it, it will cause confusion.

- Your mind will not complement the way your healing will come.

- The spirit of Elijah gives us the ability to see things that are far off, come nigh.

- When you are made whole you begin to understand Him more than you ever have before.

- Justification is an act of deception that will leave you empty.

- Receiving knowledge and understanding of the glory of God will fill you as the water covers the seas.

- Understand that, "Deception is the counterfeit of the truth".

- Perception if based in deception, brings forth misconception.

- He is the God of all wonders, but He won't leave you wondering.

- In order to destroy distraction, you simply change positions.

- Premature death entertains the enemy.

- Contentment is the counterfeit to peace.

- Justification is an act of deception that will leave you empty.

- Meltdowns are evidence of change occuring.

- You receive revelation automatically when you make yourself available to go out not knowing where you are going.

- Pain is the counterfeit of power. Your power will overcome your pain as you give it permission.

- We can't resent or resist the opportunity of being hurt because pain is an expression of what is about to come to pass.

- It's the pain of our past that makes us available to brokenness; the pain of the past has to stop before we can walk in present day wholeness.

- Pride stops you from hearing God.

- Pride will bring destruction and poverty to your life.

- Humility respects and honors sovereignty.

- Don't let what other people want confuse you. Don't let other people's lack of knowledge steal your intelligence.

- The word BUT has the power to cancel your faith!

- Some of the things in which we say we understand is really misunderstanding. It's okay to be wrong.

- Knowing where you are is the evidence of realizing where you have been.

- Things that you cannot identify will have authority over you.

- Justification will disqualify you from sanctification.

- Justification will also keep you away from glorification.

- When you don't tolerate unnecessary chaos and confusion any longer, you can reach sanctification.

- Religion is the enemy to relationships.

- You duplicate whatever influences you.

- Discernment dislodges you from the place you have been stuck prophetically, and moves you into the revelatory where you can see the unseen.

- Being in the wrong position will disqualify you from receiving restoration.

- Religion is for takers, Revelation is for givers.

- Wisdom brings automatic authority.

- We need to understand that if we want to walk in authority, we must not nag. The Webster's definition to 'nag' is "to annoy by continual scolding, faultfinding, complaining, urging, etc.".

- We nag because we don't have answers. Nagging is the counterfeit to authority, be careful not to nag or you lose your authority.

- When you constantly don't understand things, it may be a generational curse.

- You disqualify and disable your destiny when you are in a rush.

- The counterfeit will always show up unannounced when the truth is on the way.

- Our thoughts have the power to change our DNA (as a man thinketh in his heart, so is he).

- You're not afraid of the enemy, you're afraid of you!

- If we don't deal with our stuff, we die with our stuff.

- A victim mentality will convince you that you have the right to hold onto what has been done against you.

- Arise in your mentality of victimization and become victorious.

- Loneliness is the evidence of the enemy's actions.

- Pride will tell you that you are right.

- When you have the true peace of God, you don't react, you just stand.

- If it's righteousness, it will empower you. If it's not, it will empty you.

- The clearer you are on your thoughts, then you can hear other people's thoughts.

- When you trust God wholly, that's when you become holy.

- Wisdom travels with peace and joy.

- Faith is birthed out of free will.

- If you don't understand something you need to consider changing positions to make a place for understanding.

- You have to be willing to step away from what you know as understanding to understand God.

- When you are made whole, you don't tolerate brokenness.

- You can't achieve things if you don't conceive them.

- Whatever doesn't line up with the wholeness of God must be analyzed.

- Your accusations about yourself are not God's intentions for you.

- Accusations are formed out of one's opinions of past perceptions.

- Deception is an alternative to the truth that brings death.

- Two things that you need in order to carry the glory: knowledge and understanding.

- You can have knowledge but it takes understanding to know God.

- Understanding comes in the process of partaking.

- Understanding introduces you to revelation.

- Understanding added to your knowledge will make you become wise.

- As understanding comes to your knowledge then wisdom speaks.

- Understanding is making yourself available for intimacy and becoming impregnated with the glory of God

- Mary (mother of Jesus) became impregnated with Jesus by way of the glory.

- Misunderstanding of your calling can cause you to miss your calling.

- Knowledge has the power to destroy you if understanding isn't part of the equation.

- The soldiers crucified Jesus Christ with their knowledge of God, but understanding came as a result of the crucifixion.

- Wisdom is the intellect of God.

- If we don't have God's wisdom we cannot reflect His intellect.

- Wisdom is no more than knowledge matured with understanding. Maturation is the nature of man succumbing to the glory of God.

- Wisdom has to have interpretation. Interpretation comes after discernment is in operation.

- The wisdom of interpretation follows your obedience to discern.

- Procrastination is the foundation of religion.

Fears, Doubts, Rejections and Abandonment

- Our fears invite our failures.

- Don't make yourself available to your fear because that will give it power.

- Rejection is the acceptance of fear.

- You don't love God as much as you think you do, if you can't love you!

- We are called to project the power and glory of God. The enemy has side-swiped us with rejection to keep us from operating in the power of projection.

- When you doubt it causes a reaction. When you believe it causes you to take action.

- You have to be available for a vision from God to know that He is a provisional God. Your fear, doubt and unbelief will make a vision an anti-vision.

- The experience of past pains of being hurt, if not healed, will get you hurt.

- Fear is dread.

- God's revelation is on the other side of your fear.

- Operating under rejection is your unbelief and doubt taking authority over you.

- Fear is the counterfeit of courage. Courage and clarity are characteristics of authority.

- Boldness is birthed out of overcoming our fears.

- Inferiority is the counterfeit to authority.

- The winds of fear will always blow before the wind of faith operates.

- Fear that is not repented of will turn into torment.

- Torment travels with fear as an unexpected guest.

- Sympathy is best described as simple pity.

- We pity others out of our own brokenness.

- What you tolerate will terrorize you.

- What you dread the most will come upon you.

- Distraction is fear manifesting.

- Whatever you allow to distract you, will destroy you.

- Distractions come to paralyze and de-spiritualize you.

- The areas of your fears are the areas in which you don't trust Him.

- What you do, your children will too.

- Fear is the counterfeit of courage.

- Retaliation stems from rebellion and rebellion comes from pride.

- If we have fear, we are in rebellion to what God says. Fear not!

- Fear will paralyze you.

- Fear aborts dominion and authority. Faith releases authority and dominion.

- Fear works in the past, present and future.

- Mistakes when analyzed and overcome, create wisdom.

- When you are stuck in your mistakes, it is because you're living a life of regret. Repent of regret and move on to freedom.

- It is unrighteous to have fear.

- Fear, doubt and unbelief against yourself will bring division to your vision.

- You better find joy in today because what you cast away from your mind today may be your tomorrow's deliverance.

- The only things people say about you that bring offenses are the ones that are true.

- Expectations always find manifestations.

- We procrastinate our deliverance because we have found comfort in our bondage.

- Be deformed by fear or be formed by faith.

- By keeping fear, rejection and abandonment, you are keeping the KABOD (the glory of God) from penetrating your life and saturating you.

- Abandonment when agreed with breeds abandonment.

- When we call ourselves as being careful of others because we don't know if they will hurt us or not, this is control.

- Fear converts into faith and shatters the hindrances that tried to abort your portal.

- Fear limits faith and becomes a root and then faith dies and fear grows deeper.

- Fear will hold you back and prevent you from your present.

- Repented fear of your past releases you to walk in future faith.

- Unless you repent of today's fear you cannot walk in tomorrow's faith.

- If you have fear in the natural, then you can't have faith in the supernatural.

- Jesus broke the power of sin and rejection on the cross and you can too if you will take up the cross daily of repentance.

- Exchange your fear-based mentality for a faith-based mentality and be victorious.

- When you have nothing to hide, there is no need to panic.

- You either operate under peace or panic.

- If we operate in rejection, we disqualify ourselves for knowledge.

- Fear opens the door to afflictions.

- Unbelief is what keeps you from walking in total freedom.

- People's perceptions of past pains are what enables them to make accusations about others in deception.

- Your past pains, if not repented of, will cause you to place judgments on others that God has sent to offer you help.

- The fear of someone hurting you will be an open door for someone to hurt you.

- If you have fear, you have issues in your life that have not been dealt with.

- Fear is the only thing that is keeping you from being strong.

- True trust exposes all fears.

- Fear makes us vulnerable to brokenness.

- Fear causes confusion and confusion permits errors.

- The battle is in the heart. We have allowed fear, rejection and abandonment as residue to stay in our hearts.

- Under fear you cannot make sense of anything.

- Fear gives assumptions power to come forth.

Revelation, Destination and Deliverance

- Revelation is God's explanation.

- Revelation is when you know the miracle has changed you and you believe it.

- A miracle is a miracle whether you believe it or not. Revelation is when you believe the miracle and allow it to change you.

- Revelation is the uncovering of miracles in your life that have been waiting on your belief to manifest them.

- Resistance will abort Revelation.

- Reputation is a reflection of who you are but God's glory is wanting to take you from the place of who you are to the place that He desires you to be.

- You must realize the value of yourself in order to receive righteous recognition and respect from others.

- When you doubt yourself, you yoke up with fear that distracts you from your destiny.

- Revelation is on the other side of your dread.

- The glory transforms your life into your destiny. We are not location, we are creation.

- The glory will take you to a place of transfiguration and it will make you whole.

- False accusations place you outside of God's intentions as Adam was placed outside of the garden.

- When you allow your past to have power over your present, you slander yourself.

- Humility births revelation.

- Man limits you, God illuminates you.

- Confusion tries to distract you from your destiny.

- Whatever is consuming your life is the wrong fire. The fire of God will engulf you, not consume you.

- To have authority you must submit to authority.

- Knowledge is an element (expression) of God's wisdom.

- If you don't have a purpose you will stay in a voided place.

- Get to the core of who you are or you will never know who you can be in Him.

- The deeper you go in revelation is the depth you'll go to get yourself free.

- Premature death is no one's destiny.

- You can't walk in your destiny if you continue to walk in your past.

- Letting your yesterday mistakes hold your agenda is captivity.

- Destiny is precision. The lack of being precise keeps you out of your destiny.

- Acceleration comes after you're delivered from procrastination to catapult you to your destiny.

- Procrastination will enable insecurities to remain in a process instead of a completion.

- Acceleration is prophecy being revealed and received as truth.

- Being inaccurate will keep you from acceleration.

- It is impossible for destiny to operate without purpose.

- Under revelation, you never forget a word. That's confirmation of revelation.

- When the supernatural and the natural collide, fear has to leave.

- If you make yourself available to wisdom, you first have to make yourself available for deliverance.

- Judgment will divide you from your purpose.

- Revelation brings elevation to your situation.

- Procrastination clouds up visions. Completion clears up and empowers visions.

- Revelation always follows declarations.

- We have been disillusioned by the enemy's deception.

- In order to set the captives free, we must be free ourselves.

- God is tired of us exhausting ourselves and calling it Him. His yoke is easy. If you're carrying a heavy yoke it is because you're trying to do it yourself.

- Revelation is the wisdom of God expressed.

- If you don't decree wisdom, you will miss it by way of ignorance.

- A vision is something God wants to do and time hasn't met it yet.

- Revelation exposes the cause of the curse.

- Revelation allows you to hear with your eyes and see with your heart.

- Revelation has enough truth that it doesn't need a hypotheses, only confirmation.

- The more revelation that you hear, the more set free you can become.

- Revelation prepares you for God's Wisdom.

- There is no condemnation in the supernatural.

- Revelation prepares you to carry the Wisdom of God.

- Revelation brings the breath of life.

- You must receive revelation in order to be restored.

- Revelation comes in to explain to you why things are the way they are and how to get free.

- The prophetic realm waits for things to happen. The revelatory realm brings it forth.

- The revelation of God reveals unanswered questions to man.

- Revelation reveals, curses conceal.

- Daily deliverance has to be activated in order to stay in the secret place.

- When heights and depths collide is the point of revelation.

- Revelation is the revealing of the things that have been hidden and waiting for someone to hear them.

- Revelation will take you under the Word and show you things no one has ever seen before.

- Revelation can be seen just on the other side of your dread.

- The thing that you dread the most is concealing the revelation that God has for you to overcome.

- The formula for deliverance: Delight yourself in the Lord.

- Revelation brings wisdom to our ignorance.

- Relationships bring forth revelations.

- Having knowledge is a step deeper than receiving information.

- The lack of knowledge will keep you from seeing and hearing the glory of God.

- It's not about where you have been, it's about where you are going.

- Don't let the regret of yesterday abort your destiny for tomorrow.

- The key to revelation is organization.

- Revelation comes to change us and uncover us.

- Revelation uncovers hidden mysteries that have hindered us from where we should already be.

- The place where you are is evidence of where you have been.

God's revelation and glory are able to remove you from the place in which you have been stuck.

- The revelation of humility brings more revelation.

- Revelation is the final declaration.

- When God's glory light comes down, it leads you to your destiny.

- Divine revelation realizes that you need His will over your own.

- Acknowledgment is the action of knowledge.

- Complaining will keep you in a place of emptiness, when revelation is trying to take you in a place of fullness.

- Repent of complaining and be made whole.

- Revelation causes curses to reveal themselves, and not only reveal themselves, but also to reverse themselves.

- When God speaks there is no procrastination or hesitation on His part, only revelation.

A Healing, Not A Feeling

- If you're seeking a feeling, you've probably missed your healing.

- The glory of God brings a healing, not a feeling.

- Healings can change your DNA. The DNA of your brokenness has to be changed.

- Your healing has been hovering over you before you were ever broken, just waiting for you to excuse your mind.

- A feeling is evidence of your thoughts. A healing is evidence of His thoughts.

- The more pain you release to God, the more power He releases to you.

- You must release your pain for pleasure and peace to take its place.

- True intimacy is a healing that will make you whole.

- If you can't be real, you can't be healed.

- Feelings are emotional, healings are intimate.

- Deliverance is not a onetime event, it is what you become.

- Deliverance is the route to destiny.

- Sympathy is counterfeit of compassion.

- Sympathy allows your symptoms the access to stay within your body.

- Anxiety and adrenaline are counterfeits of true peace.

- What you invest in, is what you become.

- The closer that you get to God's will and not your will, the deeper the revelation will be.

- If confusion is in your life, get deeper in revelation.

- Peace empowers you to go deeper.

- It's not our abilities, it's our availabilities.

It's not about our mistakes, it is about our destiny.

- You don't know who you are, but when you know who He is, you will become who He desires you to be.

- Overcoming yourself is an example of emptying yourself where God can fill you with His glory. I must decrease where He can increase.

- Detach yourself from the way that you have always thought, to make yourself available for His thoughts.

- Feelings are unhealthy thoughts manifested.

- You keep yourself away from God because of the way you think about yourself.

- God loves you, therefore you have to love you.

- Being worthy is not a feeling, it's a healing.

- Your life is not your idea, you could not orchestrate such perfection.

- Trauma is a feeling that needs time to bring a healing.

Portals

- All portals begin at the Throne of God and are opened by the authority of God as we take ownership of our divine position.

- Positioning yourself under an open portal brings forth unrecognizable revelation.

- Portals are shafts of eternity submerging into time.

- Portals are opened when people become desperate enough to be introduced to their destiny.

- Desolation comes forth when portals have been constricted, this becomes the abomination of desolation.

- Mantles come down through portals.

- When our spirit travels from eternity to earth, it travels through a portal.

- This same portal resides around us our whole lives here on this earth.

- It is up to us either to expand our portals or constrict them.

- Ways that expand our portals: Faith, Love, Forgiveness, Acceptance, Repentance, Renewal, Restoration, etc..

- Ways that constrict our portals: Fear, Doubt, Unbelief, Hate, Strife, Unforgiveness, Contentions, Rebellion, Confusions, Judgments, etc..

- A portal is a point of contact for heaven to invade earth.

- Your portal is your secret place.

- Every time that you tell a testimony it increases your portal.

- Portals open every time a child is born.

- Portals can be magnified.

- When your portals are expanded, it automatically breaks generational curses.

- Portals offer protection. A portal encapsulates God's children. Shadrach, Meshach and Abednego were in a portal to protect them from the fire.

- Daniel was encapsulated in the lion's den by his portal.

- Desolation is when a portal is constricted by man's fear. The abomination of desolation!

- When portals are constricted, it brings premature death.

- Obedience always brings forth an expansion to your portal. Disobedience will constrict your portal.

- Procrastination will constrict your portal.

- Portals have dominion over directions.

- Portals are ways to travel spiritually.

- Portals are the entrance to the city of heaven.

- Wisdom comes through your portal as you expand it by faith.

- The rod and staff that God speaks of are symbolic of portals (guidance and protection).

- Signs, wonders and miracles come through portals.

- When you expand your portal, you bring forth: more glory, more life and more love.

- Self-bitterness will constrict your portal.

- You decide by your faith how much of God's glory (light) travels through your portal.

- Promises come to pass through portals.

- The throne of grace is the entrance to your portal. When we are born our spirit comes from God through our portal from His throne place of grace.

- Portals united with other portals bring forth the greater glory.

- Our inheritance is located within our portal.

Getting Over Yourself

- The only qualification to carry God's glory is to "Get Over Yourself".

- You can get over the enemy, when you get over yourself.

- What you tolerate will terrorize you.

- You cannot receive what you cannot handle. When you get over yourself you can handle anything and everything.

- Holy confrontation is a necessity if you are going to be free and set others free.

- As long as we are in a place of comfort, we will disable ourselves from wholeness.

- The only way to be free from the enemy is to get over yourself.

- The enemy cannot hold you down unless you hand him your thoughts.

- Compassion is when you can get over yourself and minister to others out of your own wholeness.

- You must get over your own will to walk out His will.

- Getting over yourself makes you available to see through His eyes.

- If you cannot love yourself, it interrupts the way other people love you.

- If you can't love you, then who can?

- When you get over yourself and can finally love you, God will give you revelation that the angels haven't even heard.

- When you get over yourself, you are able to live in the revelatory realm.

- When you don't deal with your issues at hand, this kind of pride will make it hard to stand.

- The only way to get in the way of your own deliverance is to procrastinate getting over yourself.

- When you get sick of something that's when you'll move and this is when you get over yourself.

- If you go back to doing the thing that you used to do that didn't work, then you haven't gotten over yourself.

- Ultimate joy is overcoming yourself!

- Getting over yourself is a daily chore that no one else can do for you.

- You must get higher than yourself, in order to get over yourself.

- You have to meet yourself face to face before you can meet Him face to face.

- When you overcome yourself is when God let's you see the whole picture.

- The evidence of your deliverance is manifested in your ability to become humble.

- When you get over yourself, you become available to hear God's revelation over your own thoughts.

- Misunderstanding leaves as your brokenness leaves.

- We hold onto our brokenness when we try to make things work.

- According to your wholeness (getting over yourself) is the magnitude of you receiving revelation.

- The things that you think in your own mind are not of your own doings, it's His revelation.

- Sometimes complaining satisfies us to the point that we don't have to confront.

- The reason that we cannot confront others is because of the lack of self confidence.

- Complaining is the counterfeit to confrontations.

- You don't have the right to complain about what you won't confront.

- If we can get free from ourselves here, we can have heavenly things here and not have to wait until we get to heaven.

- Until you get over yourself, you remain your own enemy.

- When you get over yourself, you begin to realize the power of your purpose.

- The only qualification to carry the glory of God is to be free of yourself.

- Getting over yourself will bring you out of the shell.

- The shell is the counterfeit to the secret place.

- It's the veil that led you to the shell.

- When you hold onto negative behaviors, this is evidence of living in your shell.

- Come out of whatever holds you back from being free.

- Getting over yourself means being made whole.

- Being made whole will introduce you to your destiny.

- Walking in your brokenness will detour you from your destiny.

- When you are made whole, you cannot be offended.

- The biggest part of your deliverance is admitting your wrongs.

Judgment and Discernment

- Judgment is sin.

- Judgment will keep you from receiving the truth.

- Judgment will block the voice of God.

- When you have judgment against yourself, you will never see yourself as His bride.

- Opinions come from judgments.

- If someone judges others harshly, this is evidence that they judge themselves.

- It's our judgments of others, that got us judged by others.

- We are so accustomed to judging others, that we have to be delivered one thought at a time.

- Judgment is not discernment.

- We are quick to rebuke others because we can't do anything about ourselves and this brings judgment.

- Discernment is knowing the difference in right and wrong. Mature discernment is choosing good.

- Discernment is spiritual. Judgment is natural.

- If someone is trying to control you, they need to be set free.

- Accusations and assumptions are bred from deception.

- Anything or anybody that we judge, has the power to return to us as an even stronger judgment.

- When you judge others you hold them to their past, which is also evidence that you are stuck in your past.

- We judge others for what we cannot control within ourselves.

- We judge others for trying to accomplish goals that we are afraid to set.

- Condemnation is a double-portion of judgment.

- Self-judgment will keep you from change.

- Anger is judgment on yourself that affects others.

- There is no mercy for the past. God's mercy is new every morning.

- What we don't deal with, will torment the next generation.

- There is no power in hypocrisy, there is only judgment.

- We misjudge when we don't know the answers.

- Intimidation by other people because of counterfeit relationships leave us empty.

- Judgments we have made of ourselves and others will keep us out of our destiny.

- Discernment is an act of faith that separates you from ignorance.

- Anything that you don't understand will always have authority over you.

- Misunderstanding of the truth is wickedness.

- Misunderstanding will bring forth pride.

- Mothers and Fathers are to escort children into accountability.

- If you are expecting someone to hurt you, you are really judging them and the thing that you fear the most happens.

- The weapon of discernment disassembles any weapon formed previously against you.

- If you can justify judgment, you will keep it and it will eventually cause bitterness.

- People tend to other people's business because they can't do anything about their own.

- The freer we get from judging others, the less we feel judged.

- If you measure sins of another, that nullifies your power of love.

- Sin brings forth interruption to God's original intent.

- Gossip is a form of murder and murder slaughters discernment.

- When we don't use knowledge to form discernment, we operate under ignorance. Ignorance is the foundation of judgment.

- Unconscious accusations are judgments that we place on God for allowing things to happen to us and blaming Him for what the enemy takes from us.

- If you want to abide in the secret place with God, be careful not to judge.

- When we end up in an empty place we either place judgment on ourselves or others.

- Judgment cancels sight and hearing, and that introduces us to our misunderstanding.

- All misunderstandings stem from judgment.

Atmosphere

- The atmosphere is affected by your thoughts.

- If you don't control your atmosphere, your atmosphere will control you.

- When the glory comes down, everything that you need is in the atmosphere.

- Your atmosphere awaits for what you have to say over it today.

- The atmosphere is made up of our thoughts. We can hear the atmosphere speak and it will speak what we have already spoken. Our prayers, praises, prophecies and testimonies are extended in our atmosphere. Be careful little mouths what you say!!!

- We are called to project the glory of God here on earth. Rejection will disable you from projection.

- Thoughts impregnate the atmosphere.

- Everybody enjoys heaven, few people enjoy earth.

- When you are made whole, you can see enough that you can engage the prophetic because it has been in the atmosphere for years.

- Elements of God are expressions of God. We are imagery of God. Images are greater than expressions.

- Simplicity brings forth peace.

- Man's rebellion can cause the elements which are wind, fire, water and earth to go into demonic delusions. In other words, what we don't take authority over, takes authority over us.

- Thoughts make up our atmosphere as molecules make up water.

- Wherever God hovers, His Spirit has already been. This is the deep calling the deep.

- You have to give permission to negative thoughts to allow them to become part of your atmosphere.

- When you live in the revelatory realm, you receive impregnations from revelations.

- Atmospheres are made up of thoughts and words.

- We cannot take authority over our atmosphere, unless we have authority over our issues.

- Thoughts become alive when spoken.

- When you are made whole by the glory of God, you gain authority not only over yourself but also over your atmosphere.

Pride or Humility

- Love is the foundation of humility, and it breaks the darkness that holds people to pride.

- Pride tries to justify unhealthy emotions.

- Rebellion will keep you from repentance.

- True courage comes after humility. Courage is an ingredient of faith.

- Do not sympathize with your past, because your god becomes self-pity and you put yourself on the throne instead of God.

- Self-pity is the foundation of victimization.

- Pride consists of anything that has to be covered up or concealed.

- Pride tells you that you are always right.

- Your healing is waiting on your repentance.

- You cannot be veiled by God's glory, if you are veiled with rebellion.

- Self-pity is based in pride.

- Self-pity will make you want to apologize and not mean it.

- Stubbornness is a result to self-pity.

- Anytime you think that you have to prove a point, you may want to check it out to make sure it is not witchcraft. Rebellion is the sin of witchcraft.

Generational Curses

- Generational curses are the chains that are holding you back from your destiny.

- A generational curse is any repetitious pattern of destruction.

- Repetition and tradition will disable and disengage the power that works within you.

- Judgment will cause a curse to come on you. Discernment will take the curse off.

- The very thing that you judge will come upon you or maybe even your children.

- Unrepented sins will allow generational curses to come.

- Holy confrontation breaks curses when done in love.

- Generational curses are intimacy robbers.

- Pride will enable a generational curse to remain active in your life. Break the process of pride and generational curses have to flee.

- We must analyze our past and not sympathize with it to see generational curses broken.

- Disobedience is the foundation to every generational curse.

- The presence of a curse will bring forth fear.

- Generational curses are attracted to disorganization.

- Double-mindedness is a generational curse that you adopted from others.

- Traumas are manifestations of generational curses.

- Disobedience can reopen a generational curse.

- Generational curses are real and can be broken through love, repentance and obedience.

- Generational curses torment, terrorize and place time lines on what God would like to do as blessings for His children.

- Self-pity will take you into a curse of hopelessness.

- When we continue to justify untruths and call them truths, this will cause a curse to form in our lives.

- Rebellion is the origin of all curses.

- Rebellion gives the curse permission to reside.

- Perceptions and assumptions that no one loves you is evidence of a generational curse of abandonment that needs to be broken.

Rebecca,

As I was consuming your book, I realized it bespeaks ever so deeply who and where you are in your ministry. Who could not expand their portal, wake up and passionately begin to get over themselves after experiencing this book?

We are drawn to the leap which thrusts us into the moving rope of words held between you and God. Sometimes the rope is turned fast, and we have to really want to keep up. Then the rope may slow, and we are gently loved and wooed by the pace of oneness between you, us and God. Thank You.

Love,

Brenda Aultman

Made in the USA
Charleston, SC
13 September 2013